RETURN
FROM THE U.S.S.R.

RETURN
FROM THE U.S.S.R.

by

ANDRÉ GIDE

Translated from the French by
DOROTHY BUSSY

NEW YORK · ALFRED · A · KNOPF

1 9 3 7

I DEDICATE THESE PAGES

TO THE MEMORY OF

EUGÈNE DABIT,

BESIDE WHOM, WITH WHOM,

THEY WERE LIVED AND THOUGHT

THE HOMERIC HYMN TO DEMETER *relates how the great goddess, in the course of her wanderings in search of her daughter, came to the court of Keleos. No one recognized the goddess under the borrowed form of a humble wet-nurse; and Queen Metaneira entrusted to her care her latest-born child, the infant Demophoon, afterwards known as Triptolemus, the founder of agriculture.*

Every evening, behind closed doors, while the household was asleep, Demeter took little Demophoon out of his comfortable cradle and with apparent cruelty, though moved in reality by a great love and desirous of bringing him eventually to the state of godhood, laid the naked child on a glowing bed of embers. I imagine the mighty Demeter bending maternally over the radiant nursling as over the future race of mankind. He endures the fiery charcoal; he gathers strength from the ordeal. Something superhuman is fostered in him, something robust, something beyond all hope glorious. Ah, had Demeter only been able to carry through her bold attempt, to bring her daring venture to a successful issue! But Metaneira becoming anxious, says the legend, burst suddenly into the room where the experiment was being carried on and, guided by her mistaken fears, thrust aside the goddess at her work of forging the superman, pushed away the embers, and, in order to save the child, lost the god.

CONTENTS

FOREWORD

THREE YEARS AGO I declared my admiration, my love, for the U.S.S.R. An unprecedented experiment was being attempted there which filled our hearts with hope and from which we expected an immense advance, an impetus capable of carrying forward in its stride the whole human race. It is indeed worth while living, I thought, in order to be present at this rebirth, and worth while giving one's life in order to help it on. In our hearts and in our minds we resolutely linked the future of culture itself with the glorious destiny of the U.S.S.R. We have frequently said so. We should have liked to repeat it once again.

Already, without as yet having seen things for ourselves, we could not but feel disturbed by certain recent decisions which seemed to denote a change of orientation.

At that moment (October 1935) I wrote as follows:

"It is largely moreover the stupidity and unfairness of the attacks on the U.S.S.R. that make us defend it with some obstinacy. Those same yelpers will begin to approve the Soviet Union just as we shall cease to do so; for what they will approve are those very compromises and concessions which will make some others say: 'There! You see!' but which will lead away from the goal it had at first set itself. Let us hope that in order to keep our eyes fixed on that goal we may not be obliged to avert them from the Soviet Union."

Nouvelle Revue Française, March 1936

Resolving, however, to maintain at all costs my confidence until I had more to go upon, and preferring to doubt my own judgment, I declared once more, four days after my arrival in Moscow, in my speech in the Red Square on the occasion of Gorki's funeral: "The fate of culture is bound up in our minds with the destiny of the Soviet Union. We will defend it."

I have always maintained that the wish to remain true to oneself too often carries with it a risk of insincerity; and I consider that if ever sincerity is important, it is surely when the beliefs of great masses of people are involved together with one's own.

If I had been mistaken at first, it would be better to acknowledge it at once, for in this case I am responsible for all those who might be led astray by this mistake of mine. One should not allow feelings of personal vanity to interfere; and indeed, such feelings are on the whole foreign to me. There are things more important in my eyes than myself, more important than the U.S.S.R. These things are humanity, its destiny, and its culture.

But was I mistaken at first? Those who have followed the evolution of the Soviet Union during a lapse of time no longer than the last year or so can say whether it is I who have changed or whether it is not rather the Soviet Union. And by the Soviet Union I mean the man at its head.

Others, more qualified than I am, will be able to tell us whether possibly this change of orientation is not in reality only apparent, and whether what appears to us to be a derogation is not a necessary consequence of certain previous decisions.

The Soviet Union is "in the making"; one cannot say it too often. And to that is due the extraordinary interest of a stay in this immense country which is now in labour; one feels that one is contemplating the parturition of the future.

Good and bad alike are to be found there; I should say rather: the best and the worst. The best was often achieved only by an immense effort. That effort has not always and everywhere achieved what it set out to achieve. Sometimes one is able to think: not yet. Sometimes the worst accompanies and shadows the best; it almost seems as if it were a consequence of the best. And one passes from the brightest light to the darkest shade with a disconcerting abruptness. It often happens that the traveller, according to his own preconceived notions, only grasps one side or the other. It too often happens that the friends of the Soviet Union refuse to see the bad side, or, at any rate, refuse to admit the bad side; so that too often what is true about the U.S.S.R. is said with enmity, and what is false with love.

Now my mind is so constructed that its severest criticisms are addressed to those whom I should like always to be able to approve. To confine one-self exclusively to praise is a bad way of proving one's devotion, and I believe I am doing the Soviet Union itself and the cause that it represents in our eyes a greater service by speaking without dissimulation or indulgence. It is precisely because of my admiration for the Soviet Union and for the wonders it has already performed that I am going to criticize, because of what we had expected from it, above all because of what it had allowed us to hope for.

Who shall say what the Soviet Union has been to us? More than a chosen land—an example, a guide. What we have dreamt of, what we have hardly dared to hope, but towards which we were straining all our will and all our strength, was coming into being over there. A land existed where

Utopia was in process of becoming reality. Tremendous achievements had already made us exacting. The greatest difficulties appeared to have been got over, and we entered joyfully and boldly into the sort of engagement this land had contracted in the name of all suffering peoples.

Up to what point should we likewise feel ourselves involved in case of failure? But the very idea of failure cannot be entertained.

If certain tacit promises have not been kept, what should be incriminated? Should we throw the responsibility on the first directives, or rather on subsequent deviations and compromises, however explicable these may be?

I give here my personal reflections on the things that the Soviet Union takes pleasure and a legitimate pride in showing, and on what, side by side with these things, I was able to observe. The achievements of the U.S.S.R. are usually admirable. Whole regions have already taken on the smiling aspect of happiness. Those who approved me for leaving the Governor's motor-car in the Congo, in order to seek contact with all and sundry and thereby to learn something, can they reproach me for having had a similar end in view in the U.S.S.R. and for not letting myself be dazzled?

I do not hide from myself the apparent advantage that hostile parties—those for whom "their love of order is indistinguishable from their partiality to tyrants" [1]—will try to derive from my book. And this would have prevented me from publishing it, from writing it, even, were not my conviction still firm and unshaken that, on the one hand, the Soviet Union will end by triumphing over the serious errors that I point out, on the other, and this is more important, that the particular errors of one country cannot suffice to compromise a cause which is international and universal. Falsehood, even that which consists in silence, may appear opportune, as may perseverance in falsehood, but it leaves far too dangerous weapons in the hands of the enemy, and truth, however painful, only wounds in order to cure.

[1] Tocqueville: *On Democracy in America* (Introduction).

RETURN
FROM THE U.S.S.R.

RETURN FROM THE U.S.S.R.

I

ENTERING INTO DIRECT CONTACT with a people of workers in factories, workshops, and yards, in gardens, homes of rest, and "parks of culture," I had moments of intense joy. I felt the establishment of a sudden sympathy between these new comrades and myself; I felt my heart expand and blossom. This is why I look more smiling—more laughing even—in the photographs that were taken of me out there, than I am often able to be in France. And how often too the tears would start to my eyes—tears of overflowing joy, of tenderness and love! In that rest-home for the Donbass miners, for instance, in the immediate neighbourhood of Sochi. . . . No, no! There was nothing artificial there, nothing that had been prepared beforehand. I arrived one evening unexpectedly, without having been announced, but there and then they won my confidence.

And that impromptu visit I paid to the children's camp near Borzhom—a modest, an almost humble place, but the children in it, radiant with health and happiness, seemed as though they wanted to make me an offering of their joy. What can I say? Words are powerless to grasp so deep and simple an emotion. . . . But why mention these rather than so many others? Poets of Georgia, intellectuals, students, and, above all, workmen, how many inspired me with the liveliest affection! I never ceased to regret my ignorance of their language. And yet their smiles, their eyes, spoke so eloquently of sympathy that I began to doubt whether much more could have been added by words. It must be said too that I was introduced everywhere as a friend, and what all these looks expressed as well was a kind of gratitude. I wish I could deserve it still better than I do; and that is another motive that urges me to speak.

What they like showing you best are their greatest successes. Of course, and quite naturally; but numberless times we came unexpectedly upon village schools, children's playgrounds, clubs, which no one thought of showing us and which were no doubt indistinguishable from many others. It was those that I especially admired, precisely because nothing had been prepared in them for show.

The children in all the pioneer camps I visited

are handsome, well fed (five meals a day), well cared for—made much of, even—and merry. Their eyes are frank and trustful; their laughter has nothing spiteful or malicious in it; they might well have thought us foreigners rather ridiculous; not for a moment did I catch in any one of them the slightest trace of mockery.

This same look of open-hearted happiness is often to be seen too among their elders, who are as handsome, as vigorous, as the children. The "parks of culture" where they meet in the evening after the day's work is over are unquestionable successes; the finest of them all is the one at Moscow.

I used to go there often. It is a pleasure-resort, something like a Luna Park on an immense scale. Once inside the gates, you feel yourself in a foreign land. These crowds of young men and women behave with propriety, with decency; not the slightest trace of stupid or vulgar foolery, of rowdiness, of licentiousness, or even of flirtation. The whole place is pervaded with a kind of joyous ardour. In one spot you find games being organized; in another, dances; they are generally started, led, and directed by a man or woman captain, and are carried out with perfect order. Immense chains are formed in which anyone may join, but there are always many more spectators than performers. In another place there are popular dances and songs, accompanied usually by a simple accordion. Else-

where, in an enclosure, to which nevertheless the
access is free, the devotees of physical exercise show
their acrobatic skill in various ways; a professional
trainer superintends the more dangerous move-
ments, advises, and guides; farther on are gymnastic
apparatus, bars and ropes; everyone awaits his turn
patiently with mutual encouragements. A large
space of ground is reserved for volley-ball; and I
never tired of watching the strength, grace, and skill
of the players. Farther on, you come upon the sec-
tion of quiet amusements—chess, chequers, and
quantities of trifling games which demand skill or
patience; some of these were unfamiliar to me and
extremely ingenious, as were many other devices
for exercising strength, suppleness, or agility which
I had never seen and cannot attempt to describe,
though certainly some of them would become popular with us. Enough occupations were here to fill
hours of one's time. Some were for adults, some for
children. The smallest of these latter have their
own separate domain where they are supplied with
little houses, little boats, little motor-cars, and
quantities of little tools adapted to their size. In a
broad path following on from the quiet games
(there are so many candidates for these that sometimes you have to wait a long time before finding
a free table), wooden boards are set up on which
are posted all sorts of riddles, puzzles, and problems.
All this, I repeat, without the smallest vulgarity;

these immense crowds behave with perfect propriety and are manifestly inspired with good feeling, dignity, and decorum—and that, too, without any effort and as a matter of course. The public, without counting the children, is almost entirely composed of working people who come there for sports-training, amusement, or instruction (for reading-rooms, lecture-rooms, cinemas, libraries, etc., are also provided, and there are bathing-pools on the Moskva). Here and there too, in the immense park, you come upon a miniature platform where an impromptu professor is haranguing—giving object-lessons, or instruction in history or geography, accompanied by blackboard illustrations—sometimes even in medicine or physiology, with copious reference to anatomical plates. Everybody listens with intense seriousness. I have already said that I never anywhere caught the smallest attempt at mockery.[1]

But here is something better still—a little outdoor theatre, the auditorium of which is packed with some five hundred spectators, listening in religious silence to an actor who is reciting Pushkin (parts of *Eugene Onegin*). In another corner of the

[1] "And you think that a good thing?" cried my friend X, when I told him this. "Mockery, irony, criticism are all of a piece. The child who is incapable of making fun will turn into the credulous and submissive youth whom later on you, my dear mocker, will criticize for his '*conformism*.' Give me French banter—even if I'm the one to suffer from it."

park, near the entrance, is the parachute ground. This is a sport which is highly appreciated in the U.S.S.R. Every two minutes or so, one of the three parachutes is launched from the top of a tower some hundred and thirty feet high and lands its occupant somewhat roughly on the ground. On with you! Who'll venture next? Volunteers press forward, wait for their turn, line up in queues. And still I haven't mentioned the great open-air theatre where, for certain performances, close upon twenty thousand spectators assemble.

The Moscow park of culture is the largest and best provided with various attractions; the one in Leningrad is the most beautiful. But every town in the Soviet Union now possesses a park of culture, besides children's playgrounds and gardens.

I also visited of course a good many factories. I know and constantly say to myself that the prosperity and happiness of the generality depend on their good management. But I am not qualified to speak of this. It has been done by others, to whose encomiums I refer you. My domain is the psychological side of things; it is of this especially—of this almost solely—that I mean to treat. If I glance indirectly at social questions, it will still be from a psychological point of view.

With increasing years, I feel less, far less, interested in scenery, however beautiful, and more and more in men. The peoples of the Soviet Union are admirable—those of Georgia, of Kakhetia, of Abkhasia, of Ukraine (I mention only those I saw), and even more so to my mind, those of Leningrad and the Crimea.

I was present in Moscow at the Festival of Youth in the Red Square. The ugliness of the buildings opposite the Kremlin was concealed by a mask of streamers and greenery. The whole thing was splendid and even—I make haste to say it here, for I shan't always be able to—in perfect taste. The admirable youth of the Soviet Union, gathered together from the north and south, from the east and west, were here on parade. The march past lasted for hours. I had never imagined so magnificent a sight. These perfect forms had evidently been trained, prepared, selected; but how can one fail to admire a country and a régime capable of producing them?

I had seen the Red Square a few days previously on the occasion of Gorki's funeral. I had seen the same people, the same and yet how different!—more like, I imagine, the Russians of the time of the Tzars. They filed past the catafalque in the great Hall of Columns uninterruptedly, interminably. This time they did not consist of the handsomest, the strongest, the most joyful representatives of the Soviet peoples, but of an indiscriminate concourse of suffering humanity—women, children (children especially), old people sometimes, nearly all of them badly dressed and some looking in the depths of poverty. A silent, dreary, respectful, and perfectly orderly procession which seemed to have come up out of the past—a procession which lasted certainly much longer than the other, glorious one. I too stayed there a long time watching them. What was Gorki to all these people? I can hardly imagine. A master? A comrade? A brother? At any rate, someone who was dead. And on all these faces—even on those of the youngest children—was imprinted a sort of melancholy stupor, but also, but above all, a force, a radiance of sympathy. There was no question here of physical beauty, but how many of the poor people I watched passing by presented me a vision of something more admirable than beauty—how many I should have liked to press to my heart!

Nowhere, indeed, is contact with any and everyone so easily established, so immediately, so deeply, so warmly, as in the U.S.S.R. There are woven in a moment—sometimes a single look suffices—ties of passionate sympathy. Yes, I think that nowhere is the feeling of a common humanity so profoundly, so strongly felt as in the U.S.S.R. In spite of the difference of language, I had never anywhere felt myself so fully a comrade, a brother; and that is worth more to me than the finest scenery in the world.

And yet I will speak of the scenery too, but not

till I have related our first meeting with a party of Komsomols.[1]

It was in the train that was taking us from Moscow to Ordzhonikidze (formerly Vladikavkaz). It is a long journey. Michael Koltzov, in the name of the Union of Soviet Writers, had put a very comfortable special car at our disposal. All six of us —Jef Last, Guilloux, Herbart, Schiffrin, Dabit, and myself, together with our woman interpreter, faithful comrade Bola—were settled in unlooked-for comfort. Besides our compartments of sleeping-berths, we had at our disposal a car which we could use as a sitting-room and in which our meals were served. Nothing could have been better. But what we didn't like so much—what we didn't like at all— was that we were unable to communicate with the rest of the train. At the first stopping-place we had got out on the platform and assured ourselves that a particularly delightful company occupied the next-door car to ours—a holiday party of Komsomols on their way to the Caucasus, with the intention of scaling Mount Kazbek. We at last managed to get the dividing doors opened and there and then got into touch with our charming neighbours. I had brought with me from Paris a number of little toys necessitating patience and a steady hand (variations of the old game of pigs in clover), and very different

[1] Communist youth.

from anything that is to be found in the U.S.S.R.
They help me on occasion to get into touch with
people whose language I don't know. These toys
were passed round. Young men and girls tried their
hands at them and weren't satisfied till they had
vanquished every difficulty. "A Komsomol," they
said, laughing, "will never allow himself to be
beaten." Their railway car was small and stuffy and
the day was particularly hot; we were all stifling,
squashed up against each other as tight as could be;
it was delightful.

I should say that to a good many of them I was
not altogether a stranger. Some of them had read
one or two of my books (generally *Travels in the
Congo*) and as, after my speech in the Red Square,
all the papers had published my photograph,
they at once recognized me and seemed extremely
touched by the interest I showed in them, though
no more than I myself was by the expression of their
sympathy. An animated argument soon arose. Jef
Last, who understands Russian very well and speaks
it too, explained that they thought the little toys
I had introduced were charming, but they won-
dered whether it was quite becoming that a man
like André Gide should enjoy playing with them.
Jef Last had to pretend that this little relaxation
served as a rest for my grey cells. For a true Komsomol is always bent on service and judges everything
from the point of view of its utility. Oh! without

pedantry, and this discussion itself was interlarded with laughter and carried on in a spirit of fun. But as there was a considerable lack of fresh air in their car, we invited a dozen or so of them to come through into ours, and the evening was spent in singing and even dancing their country songs and dances; there was enough room in our car to allow of this. This evening remains one of the most delightful memories of our journey, both for my companions and myself. And we doubt whether in any other country such sudden and natural cordiality could be met with, whether the youth of any other country is so charming.[1]

I have said that I was less interested in the scenery. And yet I should like to say something of the wonderful Caucasian forests—the one that lies on the outskirts of Kakhetia, the one in the neighbourhood of Batum, and especially the one above Borzhom in Bakuriani; it seems impossible to conceive —certainly I had never seen any more beautiful. No underwoods hide the great columns of the timber; forests, interspersed with mysterious glades, where evening falls before the day's end and where one

[1] Another thing I especially liked in the U.S.S.R. is the extraordinary prolongation of youth, which, particularly in France (but I think in all Latin countries), we are very little accustomed to. Youth is rich in promise. A boy among us soon ceases to promise in order to perform. Already at fourteen years old, everything in him becomes stereotyped. Wonder at life is no longer to be seen on his face, nor the slightest ingenuousness. The child becomes a young man without transition. Playtime is over. *Les jeux sont faits*.

can imagine Hop o' My Thumb losing himself! We passed through this marvellous forest on our way to a mountain lake which, we were told as an honour, no foreigners had ever visited before us. There was no need of that to make me admire it. On its treeless shores is a strange little village (Tabatz-kuri) which lies buried under snow for nine months of the year, and which I should have liked to describe. . . . Oh! to have been there as a simple tourist! Or as a naturalist, overjoyed at recognizing on those high plateaux the "Caucasian scabious" of my garden! . . . But it is not for this that I travelled to the U.S.S.R. The important thing for me here is man—men—what can be done with them, and what *has* been done. The forest that attracts me, the frightful tangle in which I am lost, is the forest of social questions. In the U.S.S.R. they solicit you, press on you, oppress you on every side.

2

I saw very little of the new quarters of Leningrad. In Leningrad it is St. Petersburg that I admire. I know no more beautiful city; no more harmonious blending of stone, metal,[1] and water. It might be a dream of Pushkin's or of Baudelaire's. Sometimes too it reminds one of Chirico's pictures. The buildings are perfectly proportioned like the themes of a Mozart symphony. *"Là tout n'est qu'ordre et beauté."* The mind moves in it easily and happily.

I have no inclination for the moment to speak of that prodigious picture-gallery, the Hermitage; nothing I could say about it would satisfy me. And yet I should like in passing to give a word of praise to the activity and intelligence which, whenever possible, have grouped round each picture everything by the same master that may help us to understand it—sketches, drawings, and studies which explain the work's slow formation.

On returning to it from Leningrad, Moscow

[1] Copper domes and golden spires.

strikes one as being all the more ill favoured. It actually has an oppressive and depressing effect on one's spirits. The buildings, with a few rare exceptions, are ugly (not only the very modern ones) and take no account the one of the other. I quite realize that Moscow is changing from month to month and is a town in process of formation; everything goes to prove it and everywhere one is conscious of this state of transition. But I am afraid it has started badly. On all sides buildings are being cut through, pulled down, undermined, suppressed, rebuilt, and all apparently at haphazard. But Moscow, in spite of its ugliness, remains an eminently engaging city; it is supremely alive. Let us stop looking at the houses. What interests me here is the crowd.

During the summer months almost everyone is dressed in white. Everyone is like everyone else. In no other place is the result of social levelling so obvious as in the streets of Moscow—a classless society of which every member seems to have the same needs as every other. I exaggerate a little, but not much. There is an extraordinary uniformity in people's dress; no doubt it would be equally apparent in their minds, if one could see them. This too is what enables everyone to be and to look cheerful. (People have for so long been without almost everything that very little contents them. When one's neighbour is no better off than oneself, one puts up with what one has got.) It is only after a searching study that differences become visible. At first sight the individual is sunk in the mass and so little particularized that one feels as though in speaking of people here one ought to use a collective singular and say not: "Here are men," but: "Here is some man." (As one says: "Here is some fruit," and not: "Here are fruits.")

Into this crowd I plunge; I take a bath of humanity.

What are those people doing in front of that shop? They are lined up in a queue—a queue that stretches as far as the next street. There are two to three hundred of them waiting very calmly and patiently. It is still very early. The shop has not yet opened. Three quarters of an hour later I pass by again; the same crowd is still there. I inquire with astonishment what is the use of their coming so long beforehand? What do they gain by it?

"What do they gain by it? Why, only the first-comers are served."

Then I learn that the newspapers have announced a large arrival of—I forget what (I think that day it was pillows). There are perhaps four or five hundred articles for which there will be eight or ten or fifteen hundred would-be buyers. Long before evening not one of the articles will be left over. The needs are so great and the public so numerous that the demand for a long time to come will be greater than the supply—much greater. Impossible to satisfy it.

A few hours later I went into this shop. It is enormous. Inside the crush is unbelievable. The servers, however, do not lose their heads, for no one about them shows the least sign of impatience; everybody awaits his or her turn, seated or standing, sometimes carrying a child. There is no device for taking them in order and yet there is no confusion. The whole morning and, if necessary, the whole day will be spent there, in an atmosphere which to a person coming in from the outside seems asphyxiating; then one gets accustomed to it, as one gets accustomed to everything. I was going to say one becomes resigned. But the Russians are much more than resigned; they seem to enjoy waiting—and to keep you waiting with enjoyment.

Making my way through the crowd or carried along with it, I visited the shop from top to bottom and from end to end. The goods are hardly less than repulsive. You might almost think that the stuffs, objects, etc., were deliberately made as unattractive as possible in order to put people off, so that they shall only buy out of extreme necessity and never because they are tempted. I should have liked to bring back a few souvenirs for some of my friends; everything is frightful. And yet for some months past great efforts have been made—efforts directed towards an improvement of quality; and by looking carefully and devoting the necessary time to it one can manage to discover here and there some recent articles which are quite pleasing and of some promise for the future. But before considering the quality, the quantity must first of all be sufficient, and for a long time it was not sufficient; it now just manages to be so, but only just. For that matter, the peoples of the U.S.S.R. seem to be delighted with any novelties that are offered them, even those which to our Western eyes are frightful. Intensified production will soon, I hope, permit of selection and choice; articles of better quality will continue to increase in number, and those that are inferior be progressively eliminated.

The effort towards an improvement of quality is particularly directed to food. Much still remains to be done in this field. But when we deplored the bad quality of some of the provisions, Jef Last, who was on his fourth visit to the U.S.S.R., and whose last stay there took place two years ago, marvelled, on the contrary, at the immense progress that had recently been made. The vegetables and fruit in particular are, with a few rare exceptions, if not actually bad, at any rate mediocre. Here, as everywhere else, what is delicious is swamped by what is common; that is, by what is most abundant. A prodigious quantity of melons—but they are tasteless. The impertinent Persian proverb, which I am obliged to quote in English, for I have never heard it in any other tongue: "Women for duty, boys for pleasure, melons for delight," would be misapplied here. The wine is often good (I remember in particular some delicious vintages of Tzinandali, in Kakhetia); the beer is passable. Some of the smoked fish is excellent, but will not bear travelling.

As long as necessities were lacking, it would have been unreasonable to take thought for superfluities. If more has not been done, or done sooner, in the U.S.S.R. to minister to the pleasures of appetite, it is because so many appetites were still starving.

Taste, moreover, can only become refined if comparisons are possible; and no choice was possible. No "X's beer is best." Here you are obliged to choose what is offered you. Take it or leave it. From the moment that the State is at once the maker, buyer, and seller of everything, improvement of quality can only come with improvement of culture.

Then, in spite of my anti-capitalism, I think of all those in our own country, from the great manufacturer to the small trader, who are continually racking their brains to invent some way of flattering the public taste. With what astuteness, with what subtlety, each of them applies himself to discovering some refinement that will supplant a rival. The State heeds none of this, for the State has no rival. Quality? Why trouble about it, we were asked, since there is no competition? In this way the bad quality of everything in the U.S.S.R., together with the want of public taste, is given a too facile explanation. Even if the public had good taste, they could not satisfy it. No; progress in this respect depends not so much on competition as on a more exacting demand, which culture will increasingly develop in the future. In France it would all go quicker, for in France the exacting demand already exists.

But there is another thing. Each of the Soviet states had once its popular art. What has become of them? For a long time a powerful equalitarian tendency deliberately ignored them. But these regional arts are coming back again into favour, and at the present moment they are being protected and revived, and their unique value seems beginning to be understood. Should it not be the work of an intelligent directing body to bring back into use once more the old patterns of printed stuffs, for instance, and impose them, offer them, at any rate, to the public? Nothing could be more stupidly bourgeois, more lower middle class, than the present-day productions. The displays in the shop windows of Moscow are horrifying. Whereas in old times the printed cloths, stencilled for the most part, were often very beautiful. And it was popular art, but the work of craftsmen.

To return to the people of Moscow. What strikes
one first is their extraordinary indolence. Laziness
is, I suppose, too strong a word. . . . But Stakhanovism is a marvellous invention for brisking up idle-
ness (in old days there was the knout). Stakhanovism would be useless in a country where the
workers all work. But out there, as soon as they are
left alone, they become slack. And it's a marvel how,
in spite of this, everything somehow gets done. At
the expense of what efforts from above it would be
impossible to say. In order to realize the immensity
of these efforts, one would first of all have to esti-
mate the natural unproductivity of the Russian people.

In one of the factories we visited, which was in
marvellous working order (not that I know anything about it; I admired the machines in blind
confidence; but I went into whole-hearted ecstasies
over the dining-hall, the workmen's club, their
lodgings, and all the things that have been done for
their comfort, their instruction, and their pleasure),
I was introduced to a Stakhanovite whose huge portrait I had seen posted on a wall. He had succeeded,
I was told, in doing the work of eight days in five
hours (or else the work of five days in eight hours;
I forget which). I ventured to ask whether this
didn't mean that to begin with he had spent eight
days in doing the work of five hours? But my question was not very well received and they thought

best to leave it unanswered.

I have heard tell that a party of French miners who were travelling in the U.S.S.R. went to look over one of the mines. In a spirit of good fellowship they asked to relieve a shift of Soviet miners and then and there, without putting themselves out in the least, and without even being aware of it, turned out to be Stakhanovites.

One wonders what a Soviet régime might not succeed in doing if it had workmen like ours, with their French temperament, their zeal, their conscientiousness, and their education.

It is only fair to add to this drab background that, as well as the Stakhanovites, there is a whole generation of keen and ardent youth—a joyous ferment—a yeast well able to raise and lighten the dough.

This inertia of the masses seems to me to have been, and still to be, one of the most important, one of the gravest elements of the problem Stalin had to solve. This accounts for the shock workers (Udarniks); this accounts for Stakhanovism. And the return to unequal salaries is explained by this.

We visited a model kolkhoz in the neighbourhood of Sukhum. It dates from six years back. After having struggled obscurely for some time, it is now one of the most prosperous in the country. It is known as "the millionaire," and is bursting with life and happiness. This kolkhoz stretches over a very large tract of country. The climate ensures a luxuriant vegetation. The dwelling-houses, built of wood and standing on stilts to keep them from the soil, are picturesque and charming; each one is surrounded by a fairly large garden full of fruit-trees, vegetables, and flowers. This kolkhoz succeeded last year in realizing extraordinarily big profits, which made it possible to set aside a considerable reserve fund and enabled the rate of the daily wage to be raised to sixteen and a half roubles. How is this sum fixed? By exactly the same calculations that would settle the amount of the dividends to be distributed among the stockholders if the kolkhoz were a capitalist agricultural concern. So much has been definitely gained; the exploitation of the greater number for the benefit of the few no longer exists in the Soviet Union. This is an immense advance. There are no stockholders; the workmen themselves share the profits without any contribution to the State.[1] This would be perfect, if there were no other kolkhozes which were poor and unable to make two ends meet. For if I understood rightly, each kolkhoz is autonomous and there is no question of mutual

[1] This at least is what I was repeatedly told. But I consider all "information" that has not been verified as subject to suspicion, like that given one in the colonies. I find it difficult to believe that this kolkhoz was so privileged as to escape the 7 per cent tax on gross production that is borne by the other kolkhozes; not to mention the 35 to 39 roubles capitation fee.

assistance. I am mistaken perhaps. I hope I am mistaken.[1]

I visited several dwellings in this highly prosperous kolkhoz.[2] I wish I could convey the queer and depressing impression produced by each one of these "homes"—the impression of complete depersonalization. In each, the same ugly furniture, the same portrait of Stalin, and absolutely nothing else, not the smallest object, not the smallest personal souvenir. Every dwelling is interchangeable with every other; so much so that the kolkhozians (who seem to be as interchangeable themselves) might all take up their abode in each other's houses without even noticing it.[3] In this way, no doubt, happiness is more easily achieved. And then it must be added that the kolkhozian takes all his pleasures in common. His room is merely a place to sleep in; the whole interest of his life has passed into his club,

[1] I have relegated to the appendix a few rather more detailed items of information. I collected a great many others. But figures are not my strong point and specifically economic questions escape my competence. Moreover, though these items are very precisely such as they were given me, I cannot guarantee their accuracy. Familiarity with the colonies has taught me to distrust all "information." In the next place, these questions have already been sufficiently dealt with by specialists; there is no need for me to hark back to them.

[2] In many others there are no such things as individual dwellings; people sleep in dormitories—"barrack-rooms."

[3] This impersonality of each and all makes me think that the people who sleep in dormitories suffer less from the promiscuity and the absence of privacy than if they were capable of individuality. But can this depersonalization, towards which everything in the U.S.S.R. seems to tend, be considered as progress? For my part, I cannot believe it.

his park of culture, his various meeting-places. What more can be desired? The happiness of all can only be obtained by disindividualizing each. The happiness of all can only be obtained at the expense of each. In order to be happy, conform.

3

In the U.S.S.R. everybody knows beforehand, once and for all, that on any and every subject there can be only one opinion. And in fact everybody's mind has been so moulded and this conformism become to such a degree easy, natural, and imperceptible, that I do not think any hypocrisy enters into it. Are these really the people who made the revolution? No; they are the people who profit by it. Every morning the *Pravda* teaches them just what they should know and think and believe. And he who strays from the path had better look out! So that every time you talk to one Russian you feel as if you were talking to them all. Not exactly that everyone obeys a word of command; but everything is so arranged that nobody can differ from anybody else. Remember that this moulding of the spirit begins in earliest infancy. . . . This explains their extraordinary attitude of acceptance which sometimes amazes you if you are a foreigner, and a certain capacity for happiness which amazes you even more.

You are sorry for those people who stand in a

queue for hours; but they think waiting perfectly
natural. Their bread and vegetables and fruit seem
to you bad; but there is nothing else. You find the
stuffs and the articles which you are shown frightful; but there is no choice. If every point of comparison is removed, save with a past that no one
regrets, you are delighted with what is offered you.
What is important here is to persuade people that
they are as well off as they can be until a better time
comes; to persuade them that elsewhere people are
worse off. The only way of achieving this is carefully to prevent any communication with the outside world (the world beyond the frontier, I mean).
Thanks to this the Russian workman who has a
standard of living equal or even noticeably inferior
to that of a French workman thinks himself well off,
is better off, much better off, than a workman in
France. Their happiness is made up of hope, confidence, and ignorance.

It is extremely difficult for me to introduce any
order into these reflections, owing to the interweav-
ing and overlapping of the problems. I am not a
technician and what interests me in economic questions is their psychological repercussion. I perfectly
understand the psychological reasons which render
it necessary to operate in close isolation, to prevent
any leakage at the frontiers; in present-day condi-
tions and so long as things have not improved, it is

essential to the inhabitants of the U.S.S.R. that this happiness should be protected from outside influences.

We admire in the U.S.S.R. the extraordinary *élan* towards education and towards culture; but the only objects of this education are those which induce the mind to find satisfaction in its present circumstances and exclaim: *"Oh! U.S.S.R. . . . Ave! Spes unica!"* And culture is entirely directed along a single track. There is nothing disinterested in it; it merely accumulates, and (in spite of Marxism) almost entirely lacks the critical faculty. Of course I know that what is called "self-criticism" is highly thought of. When at a distance, I admired this and I still think it might have produced the most wonderful results, if only it had been seriously and sincerely applied. But I was soon obliged to realize that apart from denunciations and complaints ("The canteen soup is badly cooked" or "The club reading-room badly swept"), criticism merely consists in asking oneself if this, that, or the other is "in the right line." The line itself is never discussed. What is discussed is whether such and such a work, or gesture, or theory conforms to this sacrosanct line. And woe to him who seeks to cross it! As much criticism as you like—up to a point. Beyond that point criticism is not allowed. There are examples of this kind of thing in history.

And nothing is a greater danger to culture than

such a frame of mind. I will go more fully into this later on.

The Soviet citizen is in an extraordinary state of ignorance concerning foreign countries.[1] More than this—he has been persuaded that everything abroad and in every department is far less prosperous than in the U.S.S.R. This illusion is cleverly fostered, for it is important that everyone, even those who are ill satisfied, should be thankful for the régime which preserves them from worse ills.

Hence a kind of *superiority complex,* of which I will give a few examples:

Every student is obliged to learn a foreign language. French has been completely abandoned. It is English and especially German that they are supposed to know. I expressed my surprise that they should speak them so badly; in our countries a fifth-form schoolboy knows more.

One of the students we questioned gave us the following explanation (in Russian and Jef Last translated it for us):

"A few years ago Germany and the United States still had something to teach us on a few points. But now we have nothing more to learn from foreigners. So why should we speak their language?" [2]

---

[1] Or at least he is only informed as to things which will encourage him in his own frame of mind.

[2] Confronted by our undisguised amazement, the student, it is true, added: "I understand—we all understand today—that such an

As a matter of fact, though they do take some interest in what is happening in foreign parts, they are far more concerned about what the foreigner thinks of them. What really interests them is to know whether we admire them enough. What they are afraid of is that we should be ill informed as to their merits. What they want from us is not information but praise.

Some charming little girls who gathered round me in a children's playground (which I must say was entirely praiseworthy, like everything else that is done here for the young) harried me with questions. What they wanted to know was not whether we have children's playgrounds in France, but whether we know in France that they have such fine children's playgrounds in the U.S.S.R.

The questions you are asked are often so staggering that I hesitate to report them. It will be thought that I have invented them. They smile sceptically when I say that Paris too has got a subway. Have we even got street-cars? Buses? . . . One of them asks (and these were not children, but educated workmen) whether we had schools too in France. Another, slightly better informed, shrugged his shoulders; "Oh yes, the French have got schools; but the children are beaten in them." He has this information on the best authority. Of course all

___

argument is absurd. A foreign language, when it no longer serves for learning, may still serve for teaching."

workers in our country are wretched; that goes without saying, for we have not yet "made the revolution." For them, outside the U.S.S.R. the reign of night begins. Apart from a few shameless capitalists, everybody else is groping in the dark.

Some educated and most "refined" young girls (at Artek camp, where only exceptional characters are admitted) were highly surprised when I mentioned Russian films and told them that *Chapaiev* and *We are from Kronstadt* had had a great success in Paris. Had they not been assured that all Russian films were banned in France? And, as those who told them so are their masters, I could see perfectly well that it was my word they doubted. The French are so fond of pulling one's leg!

In a circle of naval officers on board a battleship which had just been presented to our admiration ("This one is entirely made in the U.S.S.R."), when I went so far as to say that I was afraid that people in the Soviet Union were less well informed about what is being done in France than the people in France about what is being done in the Soviet Union, a distinctly disapproving murmur arose: "The *Pravda* gives us sufficient information about everything." And suddenly somebody in a lyrical outburst, stepping out from the group exclaimed: "In order to describe all the new and splendid and great things that are being done in the Soviet Union, there would not be paper enough in the whole world."

In that same model camp of Artek, a paradise for model children and infant prodigies, all hung round with medals and diplomas—and that is just what makes me vastly prefer some other camps for pioneers, which are more modest and less aristocratic—a child of thirteen, who I understood came from Germany, but who had already been moulded by the Union, guided me through the park, showing off its beauties. He began to recite:

"Just look! There was nothing here till quite recently . . . and then suddenly—this staircase appeared. And it's like that everywhere in the Soviet Union. Yesterday nothing; tomorrow everything. Look at those workmen over there, how hard they're working! And everywhere in the Soviet Union there are schools and camps like these. Of course they're not quite so wonderful as this one, because this camp of Artek has not got its equal in the world. Stalin takes a special interest in it. All the children who come here are remarkable.

"Later on you'll hear a child of thirteen who is going to be the best violinist in the world. His talent has already been so highly thought of that they have made him a present of a historic violin, a violin that was made by a very famous violin-maker who lived a long while ago.[1]

[1] Shortly afterwards I heard this little prodigy play some Paganini and then a pot-pourri of Gounod on his Stradivarius, and I must admit that he was amazing.

"And here—look at this wall! Could you possibly tell that it had been built in ten days?"

The child's enthusiasm seemed so sincere that I took good care not to point out that this retaining wall which had been too hastily constructed was already fissured. He only consented to see, was only able to see, what satisfied his pride, and he added in a transport:

"Even the children are astonished!" [1]

These children's sayings (sayings which had been prompted, and perhaps taught) appeared to me so revealing that I wrote them down that very evening and relate them here verbatim.

And yet I do not want it to be thought that I have no other memories of Artek. It is quite true that this children's camp is wonderful. It is built on overhanging terraces that go right down to the sea, and this splendid site is used to the best advantage with great ingenuity. Everything that one can imagine

[1] Eugène Dabit, when in the course of conversation I mentioned this superiority complex, to which his own extreme modesty made him particularly sensitive, handed me the second volume of *Dead Souls* which he was re-reading. At the beginning there is a letter from Gogol in which Dabit pointed out the following passage: "There are many among us, and particularly among our young people, who exalt the Russian virtues far too highly; instead of developing these virtues in themselves, all they think of is showing them off and saying to Europe: 'Look, foreigners, how much better we are than you!' This swaggering is terribly pernicious. While it irritates other people, it also damages the person who indulges in it. Boasting degrades the finest action in the world. As for me, I prefer a momentary dejection to self-complacency."

This Russian "swaggering" that Gogol deplores is fostered and emboldened by the present system of education.

for the well-being of children, for their hygiene, for their physical training, for their amusement, for their pleasure, has been assembled and arranged along the terraces and slopes. All the children were glowing with health and happiness. They seemed very much disappointed when we told them that we couldn't stay till the evening; they had prepared the traditional camp-fire, and decorated the trees in the lower garden with streamers in our honour. I asked that all the rejoicings, the songs and dances which were to have taken place in the evening, should be held instead before five o'clock. We had a long way to go and I insisted on getting back to Sebastopol before night. It was just as well that I did so, for it was that very evening that Eugène Dabit, who had accompanied me on my visit, fell ill. However, nothing as yet foreshadowed this and he was able to enjoy to the full the performance that the children gave us, and particularly a dance by the exquisite little Tajikistan girl called, I think, Tamar—the very same little girl that is portrayed being embraced by Stalin in those enormous posters that cover the walls of Moscow. Nothing can express the charm of the dance or the grace of the child. "One of the most exquisite memories of the Soviet Union," as Dabit said to me; and I thought so too. It was his last day of happiness.

The hotel at Sochi is very pleasant; its gardens

are extremely fine and its beach highly agreeable; but the bathers there at once want to make us admit that we have nothing comparable to it in France. A sense of decency restrains us from saying that there are better places in France—much better places.

No, what we admire at Sochi is the fact that this semi-luxury, this comfort, should be placed at the disposal of the people—if, that is, those who come to stay here are not once more a privileged set. In general, the favoured ones are the most deserving, but they are favoured on condition they conform—"keep to the line"; and these are the only people who enjoy advantages.

What we admire at Sochi is the great quantity of sanatoriums and rest-houses, all wonderfully well equipped, that surround the town. And how excellent that they should all be built for the workers! But it is painful to see next door to all this that the workmen who are employed in the construction of the new theatre should be so badly paid and herded in such sordid barracks.

What we admire at Sochi is Ostrovski. (See appendix.)

If I speak in praise of the hotel at Sochi, what words shall I find for the one at Sinop, near Sukhum, which was vastly superior and could bear comparison with the best, the finest, the most comfortable hotels in foreign seaside resorts. Its magnificent garden dates from the *ancien régime*, but the hotel building itself is of recent construction, and has been very ingeniously fitted up. Both the outside and the inside are delightful to look at and every room has a private bathroom and private terrace. The furnishing is in perfect taste, the cooking excellent, among the best we had tasted in the U.S.S.R. Sinop hotel seems to be one of the places in the world where man is nearest to being happy.

A sovkhoz [1] has been set up in the neighbourhood in order to cater for the hotel. There I admired the model stables, the model cattle-sheds, the model pigsties, and especially a gigantic hen-house—the last word in hen-houses. Every hen has a numbered ring on its leg, the number of eggs it lays is carefully noted, each one has its own little box where it is shut up in order to lay its eggs and only let out when it has laid them. (What I can't understand is why, with all this care, the eggs we get at the hotel are no better.) I may add that you are only allowed to enter the premises after you have stepped on a carpet impregnated with a sterilizing substance to disinfect your shoes. The cattle of course walk round it—never mind!

If you cross the stream which bounds the sovkhoz, you come upon a row of hovels. There four people share a room measuring eight feet by six, which they rent for two roubles per head per month. The

[1] State farm.

luxury of a meal at the sovkhoz restaurant, which costs two roubles, is beyond the means of those whose monthly salary is only seventy-five roubles. They have to content themselves with bread supplemented by dried fish.

I do not protest against the inequality of salaries; I grant that it was necessary. But there are means of remedying differences of condition; now I fear that these differences, instead of getting less, are actually on the increase. I fear that a new sort of workers' bourgeoisie may soon come into being. Satisfied (and for that very reason conservative, of course!), it will come to resemble all too closely our own petty bourgeoisie.

I see everywhere the preliminary symptoms of this.[1] And as we cannot doubt, alas, that bourgeois

[1] The recent law against abortion has horrified all whose salaries are insufficient to enable them to found a family and to bring up children. It has also horrified others, but for different reasons. Had it not been promised that a sort of referendum, a popular consultation, should be held on the subject of this law, to decide whether or not it should be enacted and applied? A huge majority declared itself (more or less openly, it is true) against this law. But public opinion was not taken into consideration, and to the almost general stupefaction, the law was passed in spite of all. The newspapers, of course, had chiefly published approvals. In the private conversations I was able to have with a good many workmen on this subject, I heard nothing but timid recriminations and resigned complaints.

Can this law be to a certain degree justified? At any rate, it was occasioned by some deplorable abuses. But from a Marxist point of view, what can one think of that other, older law against homosexuals? This law, which assimilates them to counter-revolutionaries (for non-conformism is hunted down even in sexual matters), con-

instincts, degraded, greedy, self-centred, slumber in many people's hearts notwithstanding any revolution (for many can hardly be reformed entirely from the outside), it disquiets me very much to observe, in the U.S.S.R. today, that these bourgeois instincts are indirectly flattered and encouraged by recent decisions that have been alarmingly approved of over here. With the restoration of the family (in its function of "social cell"), of inheritance, and of legacies, the love of lucre, of private ownership, is beginning to dominate the need for comradeship, for free sharing, and for life in common. Not for everybody, of course; but for many. And we see the reappearance, not of classes no doubt, but of social strata, of a kind of aristocracy; I am not referring here to the aristocracy of merit and of personal worth, but only to the aristocracy of respectability, of conformism, which in the next generation will become that of money.

Are my fears exaggerated? I hope so. As far as that goes, the Soviet Union has already shown us that it was capable of abrupt reversals. But I do fear that in order to cut short these bourgeois tendencies that are now being approved and fostered by the rulers, a revulsion will soon appear necessary which will run the risk of becoming as brutal as that which put an end to the N.E.P.

---

demns them to a sentence of five years' deportation, which can be renewed if they are not reformed by exile.

How can one not be shocked by the contempt, or at any rate the indifference, which those who are and feel themselves "on the right side" show to "inferiors," to servants,[1] to unskilled workmen, to "dailies," male and female workers by the day, and I was about to say to "the poor." There are no more classes in the U.S.S.R.—granted. But there are poor. There are too many of them—far too many. I had hoped not to see any—or, to speak more accurately, it was in order *not* to see any that I had come to the U.S.S.R.

Add to this that philanthropy, or even plain charity, is no longer the correct thing.[2] The State takes charge of all that. It takes charge of everything and there is no longer any need—granted—for private help. This leads to a kind of harshness in mutual relations, in spite of all comradeship. Of course I am not referring to relations between equals; but as regards those "inferiors" to whom I have alluded, the "superiority complex" is allowed full play.

This petty bourgeois spirit, which I greatly fear

[1] As a counterpart to this, how servile, how obsequious the servants are! Not the hotel servants, who are usually full of self-respect, although extremely cordial, but those who come into contact with the leaders and the "responsible administrators."

[2] But I hasten to add the following: in the public gardens of Sebastopol I saw a crippled child, who could only walk with crutches, pass in front of the benches where people were taking the air. I observed him for a long time while he went round with a hat. Out of twenty people to whom he applied, eighteen gave him something, but they would no doubt not have allowed themselves to be touched had he not been a cripple.

is in process of developing, is in my eyes profoundly and fundamentally counter-revolutionary.

But what is known as "counter-revolutionary" in the U.S.S.R. of today is not that at all. In fact it is practically the opposite.

The spirit which is today held to be counter-revolutionary is that same revolutionary spirit, that ferment which first broke through the half-rotten dam of the old Tzarist world. One would like to be able to think that an overflowing love of mankind, or at least an imperious need for justice, filled every heart. But when the revolution was once accomplished, triumphant, stabilized, there was no more question of such things, and the feelings which had animated the first revolutionaries began to get in the way like cumbersome objects that have ceased to be useful. I compare these feelings to the props which help to build an arch but which are removed when the keystone is in place. Now that the revolution has triumphed, now that it is stabilized and moderated, now that it is beginning to come to terms, and, some will say, to grow prudent, those that the revolutionary ferment still animates and who consider all these successive concessions to be compromises become troublesome, are reprobated and suppressed. Then would it not be better, instead of playing on words, simply to acknowledge that the revolutionary spirit (or even simply the critical spirit) is no longer the correct thing, that it is not wanted any more? What is wanted now is compliance, conformism. What is desired and demanded is approval of all that is done in the U.S.S.R.; and an attempt is being made to obtain an approval that is not mere resignation, but a sincere, an enthusiastic approval. What is most astounding is that this attempt is successful. On the other hand the smallest protest, the least criticism, is liable to the severest penalties, and in fact is immediately stifled. And I doubt whether in any other country in the world, even Hitler's Germany, thought be less free, more bowed down, more fearful (terrorized), more vassalized.

4

IN A CERTAIN OIL-REFINING FACTORY, in the neighbourhood of Sukhum, where everything seemed quite admirable—the canteen, the workers' dwellings, their club (as for the factory itself, I know nothing about such things, and admire on trust)—we went up to the "Mural Gazette" which according to custom was posted up in one of the clubrooms. We did not have time to read all the articles, but under the heading "Red Help," where as a rule foreign news is to be found, we were surprised not to see any allusion to Spain, news from which had been giving us cause for anxiety for some days past. We did not hide our surprise or our disappointment. Slight embarrassment ensued. We were thanked for our remarks; they would, we were told, certainly be taken into consideration.

The same evening there was a banquet. According to custom, the toasts were numerous. And when we had drunk the healths of the guests and then of each one in particular, Jef Last rose and, in Russian, proposed to empty a glass to the triumph of the Spanish red front. This was warmly applauded, although with a certain amount of embarrassment, it seemed to us; and at once, as though in answer— a toast to Stalin. In my turn I lifted my glass to the political prisoners of Germany, of Jugoslavia, of Hungary. . . . This time the applause was whole-hearted; we clinked our glasses, we drank. Then again, immediately afterwards—a toast to Stalin. But then, on the subject of the victims of fascism, in Germany and elsewhere, everybody knew what attitude to take up. With regard to the disturbances and the struggle in Spain, opinion, public and private, was awaiting the leadership of the *Pravda,* which had not yet declared itself. Nobody dared risk himself before knowing what to think. It was only a few days later, when we had just arrived in Sebas-topol, that a great wave of sympathy, starting from the Red Square, broke over all the newspapers, and that everywhere voluntary subscriptions to help the Government side began to be organized.

In the office of this factory a large symbolic pic-ture had struck us; it depicted, in the middle, Stalin speaking; and carefully arranged, on his right and on his left, the members of the Government ap-plauding.

Stalin's effigy is met with everywhere; his name

is on every tongue; his praises are invariably sung in every speech. In Georgia particularly, I did not enter a single inhabited room, even the humblest and the most sordid, without remarking a portrait of Stalin hanging on the wall, in the same place no doubt where the ikon used to be. Is it adoration, love, or fear? I do not know; always and everywhere he is present.

On the road from Tiflis to Batum, we passed through Gori, the small town where Stalin was born. I thought that it would no doubt be courteous to send him a message, in response to the welcome given us by the Soviet Union, where we had everywhere been acclaimed, feasted, and made much of. I should never, I thought, find a better opportunity. I stopped the car in front of the post-office and handed in the text of the telegram. This is almost exactly what I had written: "Passing through Gori, in the course of our wonderful journey, I feel the need to send you my most cordial . . ." But here the translator paused: "I cannot let you speak like this. 'You' is not enough when that 'you' is Stalin. It would be positively shocking; something must be added." And, as I displayed some amazement, they began to consult among themselves. They proposed: "You, leader of the workers," or "You, master of the peoples," or . . . I can't remember what.[1] I said that it was absurd, protested that Stalin was above such base flattery. I struggled in vain. There was nothing to be done. My telegram would only be accepted if I consented to the addition. And as it concerned a translation that I could not control, I gave up the struggle and submitted, but declined all responsibility, reflecting with sadness that all this sort of thing helps to widen between Stalin and the people an appalling, an unbridgeable gulf. And as I had already noticed that other translations of various speeches [2] that I had had occasion to make in the U.S.S.R. had been similarly touched up and "improved," I at once declared that I would not recognize as mine any text by me that might be published in Russian during my stay, and that I should say so. I have now said it.

Oh! to be sure, I refuse to see in these small distortions, which are usually unconscious, any bad intentions—rather the wish to help somebody who is ill informed as to the customs of the country and

[1] It sounds as though I was making it up, doesn't it? Alas, I am not! And people had better not try to say that we had to do with some stupid and clumsily zealous subordinates. No, we had with us, taking part in the discussion, several personages who were quite sufficiently highly placed and, at any rate, quite familiar with "what is done."

[2] X explained to me that, according to correct usage, the word "destiny" should be followed by a laudatory epithet when it is the destiny of the U.S.S.R. that is being referred to. I finally proposed "glorious," which X told me would satisfy everybody. On the other hand he asked me to be good enough to suppress the word "great" that I had put in front of "monarch." A monarch cannot be great. (See Appendix III).

who cannot desire anything better than to submit and to conform to them in his expressions and his thoughts.

Stalin, in the establishment of the first and second five-year plans, has shown such wisdom, such an intelligent flexibility in the successive modifications that he has seen fit to bring to them, that one begins to wonder whether it was possible to be more consistent; whether this gradual divergence from the first lines, this departure from Leninism, was not necessary; whether more obstinacy would not have demanded from the people a truly superhuman effort. But in either case, the pill is bitter. If not Stalin, then it is man, humanity itself, that has disappointed us. What had been attempted, what had been desired, what was thought to be on the point of achievement, after so many struggles, so much blood spilt, so many tears, was that then "above human strength"? Must one wait still longer, relinquish one's hopes, or project them into the future? That is what one asks oneself in the Soviet Union with painful anxiety. And even the suggestion of such a question is too much.

After so many months, so many years, of effort, one had the right to ask oneself: will they now at last be able to lift up their heads? They are more than ever bowed down.

It is undeniable that there has been a divergence from the first ideal. But must we then suspect that what we first wished for was not immediately attainable? Has there been a fiasco? Or an opportune and legitimate adaptation to unforeseen difficulties?

Does this passage from "mysticism" to "politics" necessarily involve a *degradation*? For we are no longer on the theoretical plane; we are in the domain of practical politics; the *menschliches, all-zumenschliches* must be reckoned with—and so must the enemy.

Many of Stalin's decisions—in recent times almost all of them—have been taken entirely with a view to Germany and are dictated by fear of her. The progressive restoration of the family, of private property, of inheritance can thus be reasonably explained; the citizen of the Soviet Union must be encouraged to feel that he has some personal possessions to defend. But it is in this way that, progressively, the first impulse is deadened, is lost, and it becomes impossible to keep the eyes fixed on the path that leads forward. And I shall be told that all this is necessary, urgent, for a flank attack might ruin the whole enterprise. But the enterprise itself is in the end compromised by these successive concessions.

There is another fear—the fear of "Trotskyism" and of what is now called over there the *counter-revolutionary spirit*. For there are some people who

refuse to believe that this compounding was necessary; all these concessions appear to them as so
many defeats. Explanations, excuses, can, perhaps,
be found for the deviation from those first directives; the deviation alone is the important thing in
their eyes. But what is demanded today is a spirit
of submission, is conformism. All those who do not
declare themselves to be satisfied are to be considered "Trotskyists." So that one begins to wonder,
if Lenin himself were to return to earth today . . . ?

To say that Stalin is always in the right is tanta-
mount to saying that Stalin always gets the best of it.

We were promised a *proletarian dictatorship*. We
are far from the mark. A dictatorship, yes, obvi-
ously; but the dictatorship of a man, not of the
united workers, not of the Soviets. It is important not to deceive oneself, and it must be frankly
acknowledged—this is not what was desired. One
step more, and we should even say—this is exactly
what was *not* desired.

To suppress the opposition in a State, or even
merely to prevent it from declaring itself, from
showing itself in the light of day, is a very serious
thing; an invitation to terrorism. If all the citizens
of a State had the same views, it would without any
doubt be more convenient for the rulers. But in the

presence of such an impoverishment who could still dare speak of "culture"? Without a counterpoise how can thought not incline all to one side? It is a proof of great wisdom, I think, to listen to one's opponents, even to cherish them if need be, while preventing them from doing harm; combat, but not suppress them. To suppress the opposition . . . ? It is fortunate, no doubt, that Stalin should succeed so ill in his endeavours to do so.

"Humanity is not uniform, we must make up our minds to that; and any attempt to simplify, to unify, to reduce it from the outside will always be odious, ruinous, and disastrously grotesque. For what is so annoying for Athalie is that it is always Eliacin, what is so annoying for Herod is that it is always the Holy Family that escapes," as I wrote in 1910.[1]

[1] *Nouveaux Prétextes,* p. 189.

5

Before going to the Soviet Union, I wrote the following passage:

"I believe that a writer's value is intimately linked to the force of the revolutionary spirit that animates him—or to be more exact (for I am not so mad as to believe that only left-wing writers have artistic value), to the force of his spirit of opposition. This spirit exists as much in Bossuet and Chateaubriand, or at the present time in Claudel, as in Molière, Voltaire, Victor Hugo, and so many others. In our form of society, a great writer, a great artist, is essentially non-conformist. He makes head against the current. This was true of Dante, of Cervantes, of Ibsen, of Gogol. It is not true apparently of Shakspere and his contemporaries, of whom John Addington Symonds says so well: 'What made the playwrights of that epoch so great . . . was that they [the authors] lived and wrote in fullest sympathy with the whole people.' [1] It was no doubt not true of Sophocles and certainly not

1 General Introduction to the Mermaid Series.

of Homer, who was the voice, we feel, of Greece itself. It would perhaps cease to be true the day that
. . . But this is the very reason that we turn our
eyes with such anxious interrogation to the Soviet
Union. Will the triumph of the revolution allow
its artists to be borne by the current? For the question arises: what will happen if the transformation
of the social State deprives the artist of all motive
for opposition? What will the artist do if there is no
reason for him to go *against* the current, if all he
need do is to let himself be carried by it? No doubt
as long as the struggle lasts and victory is not perfectly assured, he can depict the struggle, and by
himself fighting, contribute to the triumph. But
afterwards . . . ?"

This is what I asked myself before visiting the
U.S.S.R.

"You see," explained X, "it wasn't at all what
the public asked for; not at all the kind of thing we
want nowadays. Before this he had written a very
remarkable ballet which had been greatly admired." *(He* was Shostakovich, whom I had heard
praised in terms usually reserved for geniuses.)
"But what is the public to do with an opera that
leaves them with no tunes to hum when they come
out?" (Heavens! Is this the stage they're at? I
thought to myself. And yet X is himself an artist
and highly cultivated, and I had never before heard

him say anything that was not intelligent.)

"What we want nowadays are works everyone can understand, and understand immediately. If Shostakovich doesn't feel that himself, he will soon be made to by losing all his listeners."

I protested that often the finest works, and even those that eventually become the most popular, were at first appreciated by only a very small number of people. "Why, Beethoven himself," I said, and handed him a volume I happened to have on me at that very moment. "Here! Read what he says."

"In Berlin gab ich auch" (Beethoven is speaking), *"vor mehreren Jahren ein Konzert, ich griff mich an und glaubte, was Recht's zu leisten und hoffte auf tüchtigen Beifall; aber siehe da, als ich meine höchste Begeisterung ausgesprochen hatte, kein geringstes Zeichen des Beifalls ertönte."* [1]

X granted that in the U.S.S.R. a Beethoven would have found it very difficult to recover from such a failure. "You see," he went on, "an artist in our country must first of all keep in line. Otherwise even the finest gifts will be considered *formalism*. Yes, that's our word for designating whatever we

---

[1] "Several years ago I too gave a concert in Berlin. I exerted myself to the utmost and thought I had really accomplished something excellent; I hoped therefore for vigorous applause; but just imagine, after I had given utterance to my highest inspiration, not the smallest sign of approbation was heard." (Goethe's *Briefe mit lebensgeschichtlichen Verbindungen.* Vol. II, p. 287.)

don't wish to see or hear. We want to create a new art worthy of the great people we are. Art today should be popular or nothing."

"You will drive all your artists to conformism," I answered. "And the best, those who refuse to degrade their art, or will not allow it to be subservient, will be reduced to silence. The culture you claim to serve, to illustrate, to defend, will put you to shame."

Then he declared I was arguing like a bourgeois. That, for his part, he was convinced that Marxism, which had already produced such great things in other domains, would also produce works of art. He added that what prevented such works from arising was the importance that was still attached to a bygone past.

His voice became louder and louder, and he seemed to be giving a lecture or reciting a lesson. This conversation took place in the hall of the hotel at Sochi. I left him without saying anything more. But a few moments later he came to my room and, in a low voice this time, "Of course," he said, "you are perfectly right . . . but there were people listening to us just now . . . and I have an exhibition opening very soon."

X is a painter.

When we first arrived in the U.S.S.R., public opinion had barely recovered from the great quarrel of Formalism. I tried to understand what this word meant and this is what I made out:

The accusation of formalism was levelled at any artist who was capable of attaching less importance to *content* than to *form*. Let me add at once that no *content* is considered worthy of interest (or, to be more accurate, is tolerated) unless it is inclined in a certain direction. The work of art is considered formalist if it is not inclined at all and therefore has no direction (I use the word in both meanings). I confess I cannot write these words of *form* and *content* without a smile. But it would be more proper to weep that this absurd distinction should be a determining consideration in criticism. That it may have been useful politically is possible; but then stop talking of culture. Culture is in danger when criticism is not free.

In the U.S.S.R., however fine a work may be, if it is not in line it scandalizes. Beauty is considered a bourgeois value. However great a genius an artist may be, if he does not work in line, attention will turn away—will *be* turned away—from him. What is demanded of the artist, of the writer, is that he shall conform; and all the rest will be added to him.

At Tiflis I saw an exhibition of modern art which it would perhaps be charitable not to speak of. But after all, these artists had attained their object, which is to edify, to convince, to convert (episodes

of Stalin's life being used as the themes of these illustrations). Oh! it's very certain that none of these
people were "formalists." Unfortunately they were
not painters either. They made me think of Apollo,
who, when he was set to serve Admetus, had to
extinguish all his rays and from that moment did
nothing of any value, or at any rate nothing of any
good to us. But as the U.S.S.R. was no better at the
plastic arts before the revolution than after it, let
us keep to literature.

"In the days of my youth," said X, "we were recommended certain books and advised against others; and naturally it was to the latter that we were
drawn. The great difference today is that the young
people read only what they are recommended to
read and have no desire to read anything else."

Thus Dostoievski, for instance, finds today very
few readers, without our being able to say exactly
whether young people are turning away (or being
turned away) from him—to such an extent are their
minds moulded.

If the mind is obliged to obey a word of command, it can at any rate feel that it is not free. But
if it has been so manipulated beforehand that it
obeys without even waiting for the word of command, it loses even the consciousness of its enslave-
ment. I believe many young Soviet citizens would
be greatly astonished if they were told that they

had no liberty of thought, and would vehemently
deny it.

And as it always happens that we recognize the
value of certain advantages only after we have lost
them, there is nothing like a stay in the U.S.S.R.
(or of course in Germany) to help us appreciate the
inappreciable liberty of thought we still enjoy in
France—and sometimes abuse.

At Leningrad I was asked to prepare a little
speech to be addressed to a meeting of writers and
students. I had only been a week in the country
and was trying to tune in to the correct key. I therefore submitted my text to X and Y. I was at once
given to understand that my text was far from being in the right key or the right tone, and that what
I was intending to say would be most unsuitable.
Oh! it didn't take me long to realize this by myself.
As for the speech, it was never delivered. Here it is:

"I have often been asked my opinion of present-
day Soviet literature. I should like to explain why I
have always refused to give it. I shall be able at the
same time to repeat with greater precision one of
the passages of the speech I made in the Red Square
on the solemn occasion of Gorki's funeral. I was
speaking of the 'new problems' which had been
raised by the very triumph of the Soviet Republics,
problems, I said, which it would not be the least of
the U.S.S.R.'s glories to have introduced into his-

tory and to have presented to our meditations. As the future of culture seems to me to be closely bound up with their solution, it will perhaps not be amiss if I return to the subject with greater particularity.

.　　.　　.　　.　　.　　.　　.

"The great majority, even when composed of the best individuals, never bestows its approbation on what is new, potential, unconcerted, and disconcerting in a work; but only on what it can *recognize*—that is to say, the commonplace. Just as once there were bourgeois commonplaces, so now there are revolutionary commonplaces; it is important to know it. It is important to realize that the essential value of a work of art, the quality that will ensure its survival, never lies in a conformist adherence to a doctrine, be that doctrine the soundest and the surest possible; but rather in formulating questions that forestall the future's, and answers to questions that have not yet been formulated. I am very much afraid that many works, imbued with the purest spirit of Marxism, and on that account so successful today, will soon emit to the noses of tomorrow the insufferable odour of the clinic; and I believe that the works that will live most victoriously will be those that have freed themselves successfully from such preoccupations.

"When the revolution is triumphant, installed,

and established, art runs a terrible danger, a danger almost as great as under the worst fascist oppression—the danger of orthodoxy. Art that submits to orthodoxy, to even the soundest doctrines, is lost—wrecked upon the shoals of conformism. What the triumphant revolution can and should offer the artist is above all else liberty. Without liberty art loses its meaning and its value.

"Walt Whitman, on the death of President Lincoln, wrote one of his most beautiful poems. But if this poem had been imposed, if Whitman had been forced to write it by order and in conformity with an accepted cannon, his threnody would have lost all its virtue and its beauty; or rather, Whitman could not have written it.

"And as, quite naturally, the assent of the greatest number, with its accompanying applause, success, and favours, goes to the qualities the public is best able to recognize—that is say, to conformism—I wonder with some anxiety whether perhaps in this great Soviet Union there may not be vegetating obscurely, unknown to the crowd, some Baudelaire, some Keats, or some Rimbaud, who by very reason of his worth cannot make himself heard.[1] And yet

[1] But, they will say, what concern have we today with a possible Keats, Baudelaire, Rimbaud, or even Stendhal? The only value they have in our eyes now is the degree in which they reflect the moribund and corrupt society of which they were the melancholy products. If the new society of today is unable to produce them, so much the worse for them, but so much the better for us, who have nothing more to learn from them or their like. The writer who can be of service to

he, of all others, is the one who is of importance, for those who are at first disdained, like Rimbaud, Keats, Baudelaire, and even Stendhal, are those who tomorrow will be the greatest.''

---

us today is the man who is perfectly at his ease in this new form of society and whose spirit is intensified by what would have hampered the others. In other words, the man who approves, enjoys, and applauds.

Exactly. And I think that the writings of those applauders are of very slight value or service, and that if the people wish to develop their culture, they had far better not listen to them. Nothing is so useful for developing culture as to be forced to think.

As for what might be called "mirror" literature—that is to say, books that confine themselves to being a mere reflection (of a society, event, or period)—I have already said what I think of them.

Self-contemplation (and admiration) may be the first interest of a society that is still very young; but it would be extremely regrettable if this first interest were also the sole and the last.

6

SEBASTOPOL, LAST STAGE OF OUR JOURNEY. No
doubt there are more interesting and more beautiful towns in the U.S.S.R., but nowhere else had I
felt how deeply I was captivated, how lasting would
be my affection. At Sebastopol, as at Sukhum or
Sochi, though here it is less hedged round, less se-
lect, I came across Russian life and society in its
entirety, with its lacks, its defects, its sufferings,
alas! side by side with those triumphs, those achievements, that give mankind the possibility or the
promise of greater happiness. And as from day to
day the light varies, so sometimes it softened the
shades, or sometimes, on the contrary, deepened
them. But all the darkest as well as the brightest of
what I saw here drew me, attached me—sometimes
sorrowfully—to this land, to these united peoples,
to this unfamiliar climate which bestows its bless-
ings on the future and in which who knows what
unhoped-for flowers may blossom. . . . All this I
had to leave.

And already my heart began to ache with another, a fresh anguish. When I got back to Paris, what should I say? How should I answer the questions I foresaw? Wholesale judgments would certainly be expected of me. How explain that turn by turn in the U.S.S.R. I had felt so hot and so cold? In declaring my love afresh, must I hide my reserves and give a lying approval to everything? No; I feel too deeply that in acting so I should injure both the U.S.S.R. itself and the cause it stands for. But the gravest error would be to link too closely the one to the other and make the cause responsible for what we deplore in the U.S.S.R.

The help that the Soviet Union is giving to Spain shows us what fine capabilities of recovery it still possesses.

The Soviet Union has not yet finished instructing and astonishing us.

APPENDICES

I

SPEECH

*Delivered in the Red Square in Moscow on the
Occasion of Maxim Gorki's Funeral*

(20 June 1936)

MAXIM GORKI'S DEATH darkens not only the Soviet
State but the whole world. That great voice of the
Russian people that spoke through Gorki has found
an echo in the most distant lands. So that I am not
here to express a merely personal grief, but that of
French letters, of European culture, of the culture
of the whole world.

Culture has long remained the apanage of a privileged class. To be cultivated one had to have lei-
sure; a whole class of people toiled in order to enable a very few to enjoy life and to get educated;
and the garden of culture, of belles-lettres, and of
arts was a private domain, where the only people
to be admitted were not the most intelligent or the
most apt, but those who since their childhood had

been sheltered from want. No doubt it was clear that intelligence did not necessarily accompany wealth; in French literature Molière, Diderot, Rousseau, for instance, came from the people; but their readers were still the leisured classes.

When, in the great October Revolution, the deep masses of the Russian peoples rose up, it was said in the West, it was repeated, and it was even believed that this great tidal wave was going to submerge culture. For as soon as it ceased to be a privilege, was not culture in danger?

It was in reply to this query that some writers of all countries have come together with the clear feeling of an urgent duty to perform: yes, there is a menace to culture; but the danger does not come from the revolutionary and liberating forces; on the contrary, it comes from the parties who try to subjugate these forces, to break them, to hide thought itself under a bushel. The menace to culture comes from fascism, from narrow and artificial nationalisms which have nothing in common with true patriotism, with the deep love of one's country. The menace to culture comes from war, to which all these nationalisms and their hatreds fatally and necessarily lead.

I was to have presided at the international conference for the defence of culture which is being held at this moment in London. Bad news about Maxim Gorki's health made me leave suddenly for

Moscow. In this Red Square which has already seen so many tragic and glorious events, in front of Lenin's mausoleum on which so many eyes are fastened, I wish to declare before all, in the name of the writers assembled in London, and in my own, that it is to the great international revolutionary forces that must fall the task, the duty, of defending, of protecting, and of illustrating culture. The fate of culture is bound up in our minds with the destiny of the Soviet Union. We will defend it.

Just as, over and above the particular interests of each people, a great common need binds together the proletarian classes of all lands, so, over and above each national literature, there flourishes a culture composed of all that is really vital and human in each particular literature—"national in form, socialist in content," as Stalin has said.

I have often written that it is by the exercise of his most distinctive gifts that a writer best attains universal significance, because it is through being most individual that he shows himself by that very means the most human. No Russian writer has been more Russian than Maxim Gorki. No Russian writer has been listened to with more universal attention.

I was present yesterday at the march past of the people before Gorki's catafalque. I could not weary of contemplating the numbers of women, of children, of workers of all kinds for whom Maxim

Gorki had been a spokesman and a friend. I reflected with sorrow that these people, in any other country than the U.S.S.R., belonged to those to whom entry of the hall would have been forbidden; to those who, precisely, when they come to the gardens of culture are confronted with a terrible "No admittance. Private property." And tears came to my eyes at the thought that what seemed to them already so natural seemed to me, the Westerner, still so extraordinary.

And it seemed to me that there existed here, in the Soviet Union, a most surprising novelty—up till now, in all the countries of the world, a great writer has always been, more or less, a revolutionary, a fighter. In a way that was more or less conscious and more or less veiled, he thought, he wrote, in opposition to something. He refused to approve. He brought into the minds and into the hearts of people the germs of insubordination, of revolt. Respectable people, public powers, the authorities, tradition, had they been far-seeing enough, would not have hesitated to recognize in him the enemy.

Today, in the U.S.S.R., for the first time, the question is put in a very different manner; while remaining a revolutionary, the writer is no longer a rebel.[1] On the contrary, he responds to the wishes of the greatest number, of the whole people, and

[1] This was where I fooled myself; I was obliged, alas, soon to admit it.

what is most remarkable, to those of the rulers. So that there appears to be a sort of fading away of the problem, or rather a transposition so new that at first it disconcerts thought. And it will not be one of the least glories of the U.S.S.R. and of those prodigious days which still continue to shake our old world, to have called up into fresh heavens new stars and unimagined problems.

Maxim Gorki will have had the singular and glorious destiny of attaching this new world to the past and of binding it to the future. He experienced the oppression of old times, the tragic struggle of yesterday; he powerfully helped on the calm and radiant triumph of today. He lent his voice to those who had not yet been able to make themselves heard; to those who will in future, thanks to him, be listened to. From now on, Maxim Gorki belongs to history. He takes his place among the greatest.

the days of my youth, I have always experienced a
particularly fraternal feeling towards what were
then supposed to be the incomprehensible mys-
teries of the Slav soul. So much so that I was able to
feel myself in close communion with your great au-
thors, whom I had learnt to know and to love from
the moment I left school. Gogol, Turgeniev, Dostoievski, Pushkin, Tolstoi, then later Sologub,
Shchedrin, Chekhov, Gorki, to name only the dead
—with what excitement I read them, and, indeed,
with what gratitude! I found in them, together
with a highly individual art, the most surprising
revelations on man in general, and on myself in
particular. These great writers prospect regions of
the soul that other literatures, it seems to me, have
left unexplored; they instantly grasp, with delicacy,
with strength, and with that kind of indiscretion
that love permits, what lies deepest in man, what is
at the same time the most individual and the most
genuinely human. I have persistently done my best
to spread the knowledge and the love of Russian literature in France—both of the literature of the past
and that of the Soviet Union of today. We are often
ill informed, and between two peoples grave errors
and most regrettable omissions may arise; but our
curiosity is ardent, as is that of the comrades who
came to join Pierre Herbart and myself—Jef Last,
Schiffrin, Dabit, and Guilloux, two of whom be-
long to the party. These, no less than myself, hope

that our journey in the Soviet Union may enlighten us and enable us to enlighten on our return the French public, which is extraordinarily eager as to everything the Soviet Union is contributing in the way of novelties to our old world. The sympathy which you have been kind enough to show me encourages me, and I take pleasure in expressing in the name of many of those who have remained in France our cordial thanks.

I doubt whether the U.S.S.R. has conducted this anti-religious war very skilfully. It would have been allowable for the Marxists to have confined themselves to history, denied Christ's divinity, and, if they pleased, his existence, to have rejected the Church's dogmas, discredited the Revelation, and considered from a purely human and critical point of view a teaching which, after all, brought new hope to the world and the most marvellous revolutionary ferment possible at the time. It would have been allowable for them to show the manner in which the Church itself turned traitor and how the Gospels' doctrine of emancipation gave countenance (with the Church's connivance, alas) to the worst abuses of power. All this would have been better than the conspiracy of silence and negation. Nothing can prevent this thing from having been, and the ignorance in which the peoples of the U.S.S.R. are kept in regard to it leaves them without the defence of critical judgment and unvaccinated against the constant menace of an epidemic of mysticism.

There is more, and so far I have only presented my objections in their narrowest form and from a practical point of view. The ignoring, the repudiation, of the Gospels and all they have given rise to cannot fail to impoverish humanity and culture in the most lamentable way. I should be sorry for people to be suspicious of me in this respect and to scent here some whiff of my early education and convictions. I should speak in the same way about the Greek myths, which have also, I think, a profound and permanent teaching value. It seems to me absurd to *believe* them, but equally absurd to refuse to recognize the element of truth that informs them, and to think they can be treated with sufficient respect by a smile and a shrug of the shoulders. As for the arrest of development that religion may inflict upon the mind, as for the stamp that may be set upon it by faith, I know them well enough and think it right to free the new man from all such things. I agree too that superstition kept alive (with the pope's help) an abominable state of moral filth in the country districts—and in other places too (I have seen the Tzarina's apartments)—and I understand that there was urgent need for clearing the whole thing up once and for all, but . . . The Germans have an excellent image for which I have tried in vain to discover an equivalent, and which expresses what I find it difficult to say otherwise: *The baby has been emptied away with the bath-water*. The result, no doubt, of a want of discrimination as well as of too great hastiness. That the water was dirty and smelly is very likely; I have no difficulty in believing it—so dirty, in fact, that without paying any attention to the child, the whole lot was thrown away regardless.

And now if I am told that the church-bells are

fingers never ceased caressing mine, entwining them and transmitting to me the effluvia of his quivering sensibility.

Ostrovski cannot see, but he speaks, he hears. His mind is all the more active and tense that nothing comes to distract it, save perhaps physical pain. But he makes no complaint and his fine, emaciated face still manages to smile, in spite of his long-drawn agony.

The room he was lying in is bright. The song of birds, the scent of flowers in the garden outside came in through the open windows. How calm it all was! His mother and sister, his friends and visitors were seated discreetly not far from the bed; some took notes of our conversation. I told Ostrovski that the spectacle of his steadfastness had brought me a reserve of extraordinary encouragement to draw upon; but praise seemed to embarrass him; what we must admire in the U.S.S.R. is the accomplishment of a stupendous task. He is interested only in that, not in himself. Three times over, afraid of tiring him, for such unrelaxing ardour, I imagined, must be exhausting, I bade him good-bye; but he begged me to stay; he needed, one felt, to speak. He would go on speaking after we had left; and speaking for him is dictating. It is thus that he has written to dictation the book in which he relates the story of his life. He was now, I was told, dictating another. From morning to evening, and late on into the night, he works, ceaselessly dictating.

At last I rose to go. He asked me to kiss him. As I put my lips to his brow, I could hardly restrain my tears; I felt too that it was he who was leaving us and that I was saying good-bye to a dying man. . . . But for months and months, I was told, he has seemed on the brink of death and his fervour alone keeps the sinking flame alive in that frail body.

6

A KOLKHOZ

So THEN THE DAILY WAGE IS 16.50 roubles. Not a very large sum. But the brigade foreman of the kolkhoz, with whom I conversed at length while my companions were bathing (for this kolkhoz is by the seaside), explained to me that what is called "a day's work" is a conventional measure and that good workmen can do a double and sometimes even a triple "day's work" in one day.[1] He showed me the individual pay-books and the account-sheets, which all pass through his hands. Not only the quantity of work done was taken into consideration, but the quality as well. The gang foremen supply him with information on the matter, and it is according to this information that he makes out the pay-sheets. This requires a pretty complicated system of accounts, and he did not conceal the fact that he was rather overworked, but very satisfied nevertheless,

[1] The reckoning allows for a division of the "day's work" into decimal fractions.

for he was already able to credit himself personally
with the equivalent of three hundred days' work
since the beginning of the year (it being then Au-
gust 3rd). This brigade foreman had charge of
fifty-six men; between them and him are the gang
foremen. A hierarchy, in fact; but the basic salary
for the "day's work" is the same for all. Moreover,
each man enjoys the personal use of the produce of
his garden which he cultivates after having finished
his work at the kolkhoz.

For such work there are no regulation hours;
when there is no particular hurry, each man works
when he feels like it.

This led me to ask him whether some people do
not contribute less than the standard "day's work."
He replied that this does not happen. Evidently the
"day's work" is not an average one, but is a mini-
mum easily enough obtained. Moreover, the incor-
rigible slackers would rapidly be eliminated from
this kolkhoz, the advantages of which are so great
that people are always trying to enter it. But without success; the number of its members is limited.

The members of this privileged kolkhoz then
earn about six hundred roubles a month. Skilled
workers sometimes receive much more. For the unskilled, who form the great majority, the daily wage
is from five to six roubles.[1] The ordinary labourer

[1] Perhaps I had better remark that, theoretically, the rouble is
worth three French francs; that is to say, that the foreigner arriving

earns even less.

They might, it would seem, be paid a higher wage. But as long as there is no increase in the number of goods in circulation, a rise in wages would only result in a rise in prices. This, at any rate, is the objection that is made.

As it stands, the differences in wages are an inducement to skilled labour. Labourers are only too plentiful; what are lacking are specialists, technicians. No effort is spared to get hold of them; and perhaps there is nothing in the U.S.S.R. that I admire more than that the means of instruction should already almost everywhere be placed within the reach of the humblest workers, thus enabling them (it only depends on them) to rise above their precarious condition.

---

in the U.S.S.R. pays three francs for each rouble note. But the purchasing power of the rouble is hardly greater than that of the franc; moreover, many of the most essential commodities are still at a very high price (eggs, milk, meat, and especially butter, etc.). As for clothes . . . !

7

BOLSHEVO

I visited Bolshevo. It was at first a mere village which suddenly sprang into being by order, about six years ago, I think, at Gorki's initiative. Today it is a fairly large town.

It has this peculiarity. All its inhabitants are former criminals—thieves and even murderers. The master idea that presided at the formation and constitution of the town was this—that criminals are victims who have been led astray, and that a rational re-education may turn them into excellent Soviet subjects. Bolshevo has proved this. The town is prosperous. Factories were started in it which soon became model factories.

All the inhabitants of Bolshevo are reformed characters and have now become, under no leadership but their own, zealous, orderly, peaceful workers, particularly strict as to their morals and anxious to improve their minds, for which purpose all possible means are put at their disposal. And it

was not only their factories they invited me to admire, but their meeting-places, their club, their li-
brary, all their arrangements, which leave, indeed,
nothing to be desired. No trace can be seen on the
faces of these ex-criminals, in their appearance or
their language, of their past life. Nothing could be
more edifying, more reassuring and encouraging
than this visit. It leads one to think that all crimes
are imputable not to the man himself who commits
them, but to the society which drives him to com-
mit them. One of these men, then another were invited to speak, to confess their former crimes, to
relate how they had been converted, how they had
come to recognize the excellence of the new régime
and the personal satisfaction they experienced in
submitting to it. It all reminded me oddly of the
series of edifying confessions that I had heard at
Thun two years ago during a great meeting of
adepts of the Oxford Group. "I was a sinner; I was
unhappy; I did evil; but now I understand; I am
saved; I am happy." The whole thing is rather in
the rough, rather naïve, and only whets the psychol-
ogist's appetite without satisfying it. Bolshevo,
none the less, is one of the most remarkable successes on which the new Soviet State can plume itself. I am not sure whether in other countries man
would prove so malleable

8

THE BESPRIZORNIS

I HAD HOPED there would be no more *besprizornis* [1] for me to see. But there are plenty of them at Sebastopol, and I was told that there are even more at Odessa. They are not quite the same type of child as in earlier times. Nowadays these children may have parents still living; they have left their native village, sometimes through love of adventure, more frequently because they could not conceive that anywhere else it was possible to be as wretched and as starved as they were at home. Some of them are under ten. They are easily recognizable because they wear a great many more clothes (I do not say better clothes) than the other children. This is explained by the fact that they carry all their belongings about with them. The other children very often wear nothing but bathing-trunks. (This was in summer and the heat was tropical.) They run about the streets naked down to the waist and with

[1] Abandoned children.

bare feet. And this should not always be taken as a sign of poverty. They have just bathed or are going to bathe. They have a home where they can leave their other clothes, that they may need for rainy days or for the winter. As for the besprizornis, they have no domicile. They usually wear a ragged sweater as well as bathing-trunks.

What the besprizornis live on I do not know. But what I do know is that if they have enough money to buy a piece of bread, they devour it ravenously. Most of them are cheerful in spite of all; but some of them seem on the point of fainting. We talked to several of them and won their confidence. They finally told us the place where they often sleep when the weather is not fine enough to spend the night out of doors; it is near a public square where a statue of Lenin stands, under the fine portico which overlooks the embarcation quay. On the left when you go down to the sea, there is a sort of recess in the portico, shut off by a little wooden door that you do not push open but pull towards you. I did so one morning, when there were not too many people about—for I was afraid of giving away their hiding-place and getting them turned out of it—and found myself facing a small space about the size of an alcove, with no other opening, where, curled up like a kitten on a sack, a wretched little starveling was sleeping. I closed the door on his slumbers.

One morning the besprizornis had disappeared

(as a rule, they used to prowl about the large public gardens); then one of them, whom we finally discovered, told me that there had been a police raid and that all the others were under lock and key. Two of my companions had been, in fact, present at the police raid. A policeman whom they questioned told them that the children would be placed in a State institution. The next day they had all reappeared. What had happened? "They wouldn't have us," said the children. But it seems more likely that it was they themselves who refused to submit to what little discipline was demanded of them. Had they run away again? It would have been easy for the police to recapture them. One would have thought that they would have been glad to be rescued from such depths of poverty. Or did they prefer to what was offered them their poverty together with their freedom?

I saw a very small one—certainly not more than eight—being carried off by two plain-clothes policemen. Two were needed, for the child was struggling like a wildcat—sobbing, howling, stamping, trying to bite. . . . Nearly an hour later, happening to pass near the same place, I saw the same child again. He had now calmed down and was sitting on the pavement. There was only one of the two policemen standing beside him. The child was no longer trying to run away. He was smiling at the policeman. A large truck drew up, and the police-

man helped the child to get in. Where was he taking him? I do not know. And I only relate this little
incident because few things in the Soviet Union
moved me as much as the attitude of this man
towards the child; the persuasive gentleness of his
voice (ah, if I could only have understood what
he was saying!), the kindness of his smile, and his
caressing tenderness as he lifted him in his arms.
. . . I thought of Dostoievski's *Moujik Mareï* [1]—
and that it was worth while coming to the U.S.S.R.
in order to see such a thing.

[1] *A Writer's Notebook.*